I'm One, I'm One!

I'm One, I'm One!

by Valerie Carlson Pressley
Illustrated by Kayla Lynn Olson

ABOOKS
Alive Book Publishing

Additional copies may be ordered from the publisher
for educational, business, promotional or premium use.
For information, contact ALIVE Book Publishing at:
alivebookpublishing.com, or call (925) 837-7303.

ISBN 13
978-1-63132-098-9

Library of Congress Control Number: 2020912380

Library of Congress Cataloging-in-Publication Data
is available upon request.

First Edition

Published in the United States of America
by ALIVE Book Publishing
an imprint of Advanced Publishing LLC
3200 A Danville Blvd., Suite 204, Alamo, California 94507
alivebookpublishing.com

PRINTED IN THE UNITED STATES OF AMERICA

10 9 8 7 6 5 4 3 2 1

For Georgia and Logan

I'm One, I'm One! It's so much fun!
A whole year has gone by
and I'm doing a ton.

I crawl, I cruise, I walk, and I run.
Better watch out,
because here I come!

My world is now baby-proofed
—gates and locks galore.
It's not as much fun
when I want to explore.

If I get a little frustrated,
well guess what I do?
I start to make sounds
of one word or two.

I say *mama*, *up*, or *open this*!
And sometimes, just sometimes,
I get my wish.

We go to the park, slide down slides, and swing on swings. I look at the flowers and collect interesting things.

I love to dance, roll around,
and tumble.
I flap my arms like a bird.
Or like a bee, I buzz and bumble.

I'm having such fun
growing my personality.
I'm learning what it's like
to be wonderful lil' ME!

MY toy. MY shirt. MY hair. MY belly.
I want toast with no crust
and LOTS of jelly.

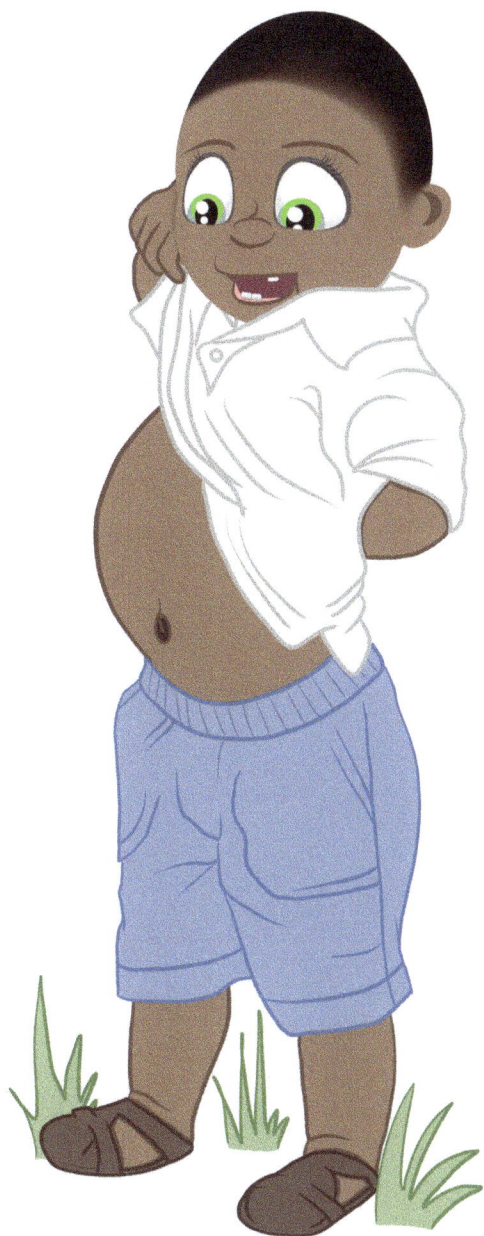

I'm determined and curious,
a budding toddler it's true.
Today I am One,
but soon I'll be Two!

Also by Valerie Carlson Pressley

I'm Here, I'm Here!
I'm Two, I'm Two!

ABOOKS

ALIVE Book Publishing and ALIVE Publishing Group
are imprints of Advanced Publishing LLC,
3200 A Danville Blvd., Suite 204, Alamo, California 94507

Telephone: 925.837.7303
alivebookpublishing.com

www.ingramcontent.com/pod-product-compliance
Lightning Source LLC
Chambersburg PA
CBHW042349040426

42448CB00019B/3474